SYSTEMS
IMPLEMENTATION
LITIGATION

SYSTEMS
IMPLEMENTATION
LITIGATION

A GUIDE
FOR **SYSTEMS
IMPLEMENTERS**,
THEIR **CUSTOMERS** &
THE **LAWYERS** WHO
REPRESENT THEM

GREG CROUSE

Disclaimer

This book is presented solely for educational purposes. The author and publisher are not offering it as legal, accounting, or other professional services advice. While best efforts have been used in preparing this book, the author and publisher make no representations or warranties of any kind and assume no liabilities of any kind with respect to the accuracy or completeness of the contents and specifically disclaim any and all warranties including but not limited to implied warranties of merchantability or fitness of use for a particular purpose.

Every company is different, and the advice and strategies contained herein may not be suitable for your situation. You should seek the services of a competent professional before beginning any systems implementation effort or engaging in litigation.

Systems Implementation Integration

©2019 by Greg Crouse

Published by Clovercroft Publishing, Franklin, Tennessee

Senior Editor: Tammy Kling

Executive Editor: Tiarra Tompkins

Copy Edited by Adept Content Solutions

Cover Design by Nelly Sanchez

Interior Design by Adept Content Solutions

Printed in the United States of America

978-1-948484-81-7

"Give me six hours to chop down a tree and
I will spend the first four sharpening the axe."

—Abraham Lincoln

Dedication

Everyone has special people in their lives, and I'd like to thank a few of mine. Thank you to my amazing mentors—including John Pliley, Moses Padron, and Tom Tynan, among others—who have kept me on the right path. Thank you to Mom and Dad, the most amazing parents anyone can ask for, to whom I owe all my success.

Thank you to all the attorneys I work with on a daily basis, as well as my team members who assist in the forensic work that makes these complex engagements possible. I am grateful for your excellence. Last, special thanks go to Scott Solomon, who has been my expert witness guide and counsel.

Contents

Introduction

Most systems integration failures involve a multitude of complex factors including poor organizational change management, a lack of clear direction, and changing priorities. Most large-scale systems implementations are extremely complicated, and many cost hundreds of millions of dollars, take multiple years, and require the help of highly trained and skilled people.

Over the last two decades I have worked with several of the largest, most complex implementations in the world, including those in the financial services, manufacturing, and energy industries, as well as government applications, and I have performed post-implementation reviews for many failed large systems installations that others have implemented. Some of these projects got back on track; others resulted in litigation.

Navigating the complexities of implementation project deliverables, project communications, and the business process behind the implementation, as well as complex technological details, can be overwhelming for even the most proficient legal teams.

How can attorneys understand the underlying processes of systems implementations as well as the vernacular of the technology landscape? Often it's the right expert witness and their advisory team that can be the game changer when it comes to litigation.

How can implementers build a solid communication plan that ensures dates and expectations are met in order to deliver what was promised and avoid litigation? If litigation is inevitable, how can the implementer or client navigate the complex process of seeking restitution?

System implementation failures often begin early in the sales cycle, and an expert witness team can help with the forensic analysis of project deliverables and communications to discover the key facts in the matter. Expert witness work is a process as complex as crime scene reconstruction and must be handled with care.

This book provides suggested guidelines, (not firm rules) since each situation is unique.

If you are reading this book as an attorney, you likely have either been approached by a potential client facing litigation or have entered litigation in this area. Or you are a customer of an implementation firm about to enter litigation related to a large systems implementation. I hope to provide some professional guidance and insight into this complex industry.

Unfortunately, systems implementation failure is a growing area of litigation that often impacts organizations to the tune of multiple millions of dollars even into the hundred-million dollar range. The size of these disputes, of course, directly relates to the complexity.

Those attorneys experienced in other areas of complex commercial litigation law will find similar themes in systems litigation matters. But I would argue that systems litigation is more complex than other areas of commercial litigation for two key reasons:

1. While there are some standard implementation methodologies on how things are done, there are literally dozens of ways to implement the same technologies. Even if an implementer does not follow an established method, they may not be doing anything wrong. Like other professional activities, sometimes the judgment of the practitioner determines which method is utilized. In other words, sometimes there is

more art than science as there is no single right way to implement a specific technology feature.

2. The tools, methods, and skills are constantly evolving. While this happens in other commercial arenas, change happens at a faster pace in technology and systems.

What do I mean by the term *systems*?
Systems typically refer to a collection of interdependent technology components that are brought together as a whole to perform a function. The systems that are in the scope of this text are typically multiple software and hardware components, which can range from two to three to several hundred, depending on the complexity of the system. Typical examples of systems are those that perform accounting functions, track inventory, or manage customer data.

This book is intended to be a guide into the complexities within systems implementations:

• As an implementer, how are communications clearly implemented with excellence in order to stay out of court, and worst-case scenario, how to best prepare when that contingency becomes unavoidable?

- As an attorney, understanding the complexities of systems implementations in general and the client's project specifically.

- This book will help implementers as well as attorneys filter out what is most important with respect to the dispute and comprehend how the litigating parties can understand one another's perspectives.

This book is not intended to inform about nuances in procedure, legal arguments, or contracts. It is also not intended to discuss areas such as intellectual property (IP) infringement. It is, however, intended to inform the following constituencies about avoiding litigation and how to determine the most critical factors to a successful implementation and advice in the event litigation is avoidable.

The topics for systems implementers as plaintiffs and defendants in this book are split into two major chapters:

- This first section, Best Practices, discusses how to keep the train on the right track to avoid litigation. Take this section as a roadmap to keeping large initiatives out of the ditch.

- The second section, Preparing for Litigation, covers considerations related to disputes that have potential to go to court. This may include discussing best practices as they relate to an arising issue or what to do as an implementer or customer in litigation.

Section 1: Best Practices for Implementers to Avoid Litigation

This section provides key points for systems implementers who want to stay out of litigation or are potentially facing litigation as a plaintiff (suing the customer usually for payment) or as a defendant (the customer is suing the implementer) prior to the commencement of litigation.

Section 2: How to Prepare for Litigation as an Implementer

This section is mainly intended for systems implementers involved in formal litigation. For implementers in litigation, this section provides some suggested guidelines on how to proceed.

Section 3: For Attorneys Involved with System Implementation Disputes

Attorneys will learn the basic concepts of systems implementation and key areas of focus during the dispute.

Section 4: Further Litigation Expertise Related to Systems Implementation

This section briefly reviews other aspects related to system implementation litigation specifically as it relates to damages in implementation disputes.

Section 5: Other Systems-Related Areas of Litigation

This section offers a quick overview of other topics not directly related to systems litigation.

Never trust a computer
you can't throw out a window.

—Steve Wozniak

Section 1—Prevention
Best Practices: Avoiding the Typical Pitfalls that Lead to Litigation

In a systems implementation matter, the best protection is to understand the pitfalls that can potentially lead to litigation. All implementers want to make their customers happy. However, unlike the customer service industry, the systems implementation customer is *not* always right, and that means that sometimes the customer needs to be given news that they don't necessarily want to hear. Being honest upfront will prevent problems and failures later.

How do we avoid failures? Many studies estimate the percentages of project failures at anywhere from 30 percent to 70 percent, depending on the study.

An examination of many of these project failures point to six common themes. These six critical areas for systems implementation success are:

1. Scope Control—Understanding, agreeing upon, and communicating the scope of the implementation, and strictly governing changes to project scope.

2. Executive Buy-in and Initiative Size—The bigger the implementation, the higher level customer executive needed as champion within the customer organization.

3. Understanding and Documenting Project Objectives—The requirements and objectives of the project should be well documented and communicated.

4. Testing Success—Test thoroughly and effectively, with traceability to objectives and requirements

5. Date Flexibility—Be realistic with deliverable dates, and allow for contingency.

6. Vendor Management—Provide proper governance of project vendors.

1.1 Scope Control

The is no shortage of clichés related to change—"the only constant is change," "change is hard," and so on—but when it comes to scope change and change management, most implementations come up short.

Scope is defined as determining and documenting a list of specific project goals, deliverables, features, functions, tasks, key deadlines, and costs. In short, scope is what needs to be achieved to deliver a particular project. These key items are usually documented in a project charter. The project charter is defined in section 3.1.4, "Sign-Offs," on page 51.

When scope is not properly documented and communicated or change of scope is not properly controlled, scope expansion or "scope creep" generally results. Scope expansion can be defined as the uncontrolled or undesired inclusion of non-critical items in the project that result in the increase of project effort or cost, or a shift in completion dates.

When scope control is mentioned, it is typically related to a change in requirements or functionality after the blueprint is set, project plans are made, charters signed-off, and so on.

It would be unreasonable to expect to avoid scope change completely, especially when dealing with complex projects that have extensive scope. A goal is to be deliberate about governing desired changes as well as thoroughly documenting changes in scope and their impacts.

Scope control is an issue across industries. While it is true that projects in other areas such as civil engineering can also go over budget and encounter schedule delays, the majority of projects do get completed, and the end product generally fulfills its intended purpose.

If the failure rates experienced in the IT sector were replicated in civil engineering, there would be roads with gaping holes and numerous bridges to nowhere. We don't see this because bridge and road projects that head in a northward direction don't normally change requirements to alter the route to go east after they get started.

In software, scope creep may result from either initial unrealistic budget or schedule requirements. Both can result in adding modifications that would affect pre-existing requirements, and if delivery dates are insufficiently changed, timeline compression can result. Oftentimes, this has impacts downstream, such as insufficient testing or unsatisfactory training.

Changes should funnel back to the agreed-upon requirements for justification, successful implementation, and support. Changes should result in requirements addendums, with documentation that ties the change to the new or modified requirement.

The goals with respect to scope control are:

1. Be judicious about the change. Ask:

    a. Can we live without this change until a later release?

    b. What are the impacts of this change at a high level (e.g., schedule, budget, technical)?

    c. Why didn't we think of this before (e.g., was there a good reason for not including this in the first place)?

    d. Does the benefit of the change exceed the associated costs?

2. Follow a consistent change management methodology.

    Use a tested change management methodology; there are many available, which will be discussed later. Or adopt the corporate change methodology in use in the customers' organization for this project, and use it consistently throughout the project if possible.

    Beware of going into "firefighting" mode: throwing the methodology out the window to resolve short-term problems. The adopted methodology should address emergency changes from the start, but keep in mind that true emergencies are relatively rare. Try not to get into the common trap of making everything a Severity One emergency.

1. Communicate the scope change broadly.

    If the scope of a project and the resulting changes in scope are communicated effectively, there should be fewer surprises about project changes to affected individuals.

    It is not unusual to have several large-scale changes every month during the course of the project, so project personnel may get fatigued about change emails by month two.

    Targeting change communications to the affected individuals is less overwhelming. In some projects, a listing of all scope changes are tracked in a "change log." This change log should be broadly published. Additionally, the overall methodology should include change management as toll-gate criteria, and these toll-gates should have input by personnel affected by the change(s).

    Tollgates are checkpoints within a project where management reviews the progress to date. These can be as thorough and critical as a root canal or focus on high-level project progress only. Additionally, these checkpoints typically occur at critical phases of the project or at preset times; once a quarter is one general timeframe. The objective is for the management team to be informed on the project's status, progress, and quality. In some cases, when the project's progress does not meet the toll-gate criteria, the project team is asked to remove deficiencies before moving forward. Occasionally projects are cancelled after reaching a tollgate, and sometimes they pass with flying colors and are completed successfully.

Key Point: Not having the proper guidance and control around scope can cause otherwise healthy programs to get into trouble.

1.2   Executive Buy-in and Initiative Size

Most large organizations are quarterly driven. Therefore, when an initiative has no payback for multiple quarters, this causes natural stresses. Couple this with a short average CIO tenure,[1] and projects are sure to get "turnover fatigue."

Humans resist change in a professional setting; their jobs may be fundamentally changed or eliminated. To combat this natural resistance, large changes should be led by an individual who is seen as a strong change agent. This should be a significantly important agent in the corporate hierarchy, and as a general rule, the larger the change, the more senior the change agent should be. It is also crucial for the change agent to be sufficiently involved with the program to set the tone for budget, timing, and scope.

The longer an initiative goes without any delivery of functionality, the more pressure is put on the team to deliver results and free up valuable resources. For this reason, multi-year projects with a single release date (aka "big bang") are advised against. In many cases, there is an opportunity to reduce project risk and accelerate some project benefit. This could happen through a quick release of improvements (aka a "quick win") or an early release of functionality to the user community (a pilot or beta test), or even an early release of incremental functionality. The odds of success are inverse to the size of the initiative; in other words, a $100-million big-bang implementation has lower success odds than ten $10-million phased initiatives.

---

1 *CIO Magazine*, "2011–2015 State of the CIO."

Big-bang initiatives are also ill-advised due to their higher-than-average complexity, along with a higher degree of difficulty to compare what was ultimately delivered with what was originally designed.

Since executives commonly want everything done at once and as quickly as possible, it is important to highlight alternatives to the big-bang approach that achieve the desired functionality without taking on unnecessary risk.

One approach can be called phasing, releases, chunks, or waves. They all mean the same thing: a large set of functionality is split into various pieces to make them more attainable. Functionality is described more in depth in section 2.4, "Requirements and Traceability," on page 27. The following chart shows some common ways that projects can be split up.

Table 1—Implementation Phasing

Type of Project Split	Description	Reasoning
By Product Family	Split project deliveries by areas of functionality. In other words, if a large system is being built for a bank, rather than replacing every system for every type of loan product, the project might split different products into different releases.	This is an option if this is a large system with multiple distinct functions, or groups of functions.

Type of Project Split	Description	Reasoning
By Geography	In this split, roll out different phases in stages to different groups of users based on their geography. This can be by country, city, state, or language.	Not all companies have multiple geographies, so this might not always be an option.
By Function	Start simple, and then grow the deliverables (defined in section 3.1.7, "Key Acronyms and Terms," page 93) to be more complex. Think of this as an app on a smartphone. The first release is usually rather basic, but by release three and up, many new features have been added.	This is common among smaller projects. It requires substantial release planning at the outset. Additionally, this method routinely results in rework. An earlier delivered function might conflict with a later feature, and will not be used in the final product. This is essentially wasted effort.
By Legal Entity	If the project involves multiple vendors, partners, or disparate operating entities, these are common areas to split into different releases. Releases are defined in section 3.1.5, "Release Phasing," on page 84.	Usually only large corporations or complex operating relationships qualify for this release type.

1.3   Requirements Criticality

Despite the numerous tools that exist for requirements management, along with the many rules about what makes up a good requirement, this seems to be another area where projects trip up. Good requirements should be:

Table 2—Characteristics of Good Requirements

Requirements Attribute	Description
Verifiable/ testable	The requirement can be tested by some objective criteria.
Concise	Requirements should be brief and to the point.
Traceable	Requirements traceability is the ability to describe and follow the life of a requirement in both a forward and backward direction. In other words, one should be able to follow a specific requirement (e.g., the systems language will be English) throughout the project lifecycle, from its original creation through to the testing of that function, all the way to the end delivery and use.
Consistent	The requirements should relate to one another and not contradict.
Complete	Each requirement contains a thorough set of criteria.
Necessary	Requirements should not be superfluous.
System Agnostic	Requirements should not call for a specific system component / technology.

In my experience, requirements in large projects often:

1. Make too few requirements (in the above chart making the requirements not testable or complete, since there are not enough of them).

2. Do not link requirements to specific units of work in the testing phase, aka test cases. In the above chart, these would not be traceable.

3. Dictate a direction for the technology. Requirements should focus on the business function and, in general, should be independent from specific technologies.

4. Are incomplete, specifically in the cases of exceptions or negative criteria. Oftentimes, requirements focus on the most common and desired path for a business process, the "happy path," and do not describe the negative outcomes. For example, take the process of cashing a check. The happy path, at a high-level, is customer presents check, money is dispersed. The exception or negative conditions might be insufficient funds, lack of proper ID, and so on.

Additionally, many organizations with large implementations choose to implement packaged (aka COTS) software. In many cases, the packages are so heavily customized that they may as well have been custom solutions, and in these cases, organizations are sometimes left with support difficulty. The elements that lead up to this issue will be outlined in later sections. For additional details about requirements, please see Section 3.1.3, "Requirements," on page 68.

Luckily, requirements management is an area where small changes can yield big results, and there are many solutions in the space. There are several tools, methodologies, and templates available. While some of these solutions are a significant investment in both time and money, these solutions usually pay off through the first large project that is successfully implemented.

1.4   Test for Success

The testing phase is the project phase where requirements and functionality are tested. The major testing phases are unit, string/integration, system, and acceptance. There are other testing subphases that are just as important but are often overlooked, specifically in the area of systems testing related to performance testing. Additionally, there are "model office" or "pilot" tests where real-life situations are leveraged with true end-users-validated usability. These phases of testing are outlined in more detail in Section 3.1.2, "The Systems Development Lifecycle (SDLC) and Methodologies," on page 58.

Unit and integration tests are sometimes performed uneventfully. Problems tend to arise in the later test phases. For example, due to either changes in schedule, additional (unplanned) functionality, or lack of staff availability, various testing efforts may be cut short and not given the original level of thoroughness. Some projects have completely skipped user acceptance testing, and some have omitted *all* performance testing.

Unfortunately, there is no single benchmark for expense allotment with regard to testing. However, it is customary to spend 25 to 40 percent of the overall project on defect testing.

> **Key Point:** Testing is usually the phase that gets compressed when projects get into difficulty. Unfortunately, testing is an extremely important phase that should not be underestimated.

1.5   Completion Date Flexibility

Dates are critical for a project's success; detailed plans that are agreed upon upfront, communicated broadly, and executed according to this detailed plan are the bedrock of a large project's success. However, if major changes occur in a project—scope changes, leadership changes, requirements changes, or even mistakes—the date may need to change.

Too often, large changes in scope are injected into a program, only to see the existing date stay the same, or worse, moved up. The reality might be that the completion date is driven by a compliance entity, or it's a date shared with shareholders or other important constituencies. If the date is critical, then don't make the change, if possible. It is difficult, and in some cases impossible, to get both a fixed date and room to accommodate changes.

Most of the large programs implemented, or for which a post-implementation review was conducted to isolate the root cause of failure, had symptoms of date compression. Successful projects sometimes deal with this is by delaying change to later releases, meeting the original date with the original scope. Likely, this will result in redundant or wasted work efforts, but this is usually preferable to a failed implementation.

Another customary practice related to scheduling and budgeting is to have an adequate contingency. A contingency line item is designed to be used for unplanned tasks and emergency items and is established at the beginning of the project. There are several calculations that are used to compute an adequate contingency, but usually these calculations result in 10 to 15 percent or more in terms of both time and budget. This contingency should be monitored closely as the use of this budget is an early warning sign of project issues.

As a humorous aside, a very well-respected software systems engineer read an early version of this book, and for this section he said: "Is this even a real thing? Do people actually change dates when they make changes in scope?" Since more than 50 percent of large programs end up as failures—and clearly in his experience, dates rarely, if ever, seem to get changed (even though most implementation programs do indeed alter scope in some fashion)—it seems the unwillingness to change delivery dates should be seriously reconsidered.

1.6   Vendor Management

There is a lot at stake in large information technology (IT) implementations. In some cases, the entire company is at risk. Most IT implementations are not undertaken by technology companies—meaning these implementations are being handled by companies that do not have a core competency in systems implementations.

This is why there are literally thousands of companies in the world that focus exclusively on implementing systems.

Consider these options to mitigate risk in hiring an implementation firm:

1. Hire your own army.

   Obtain the best and brightest implementers to manage the project and the implementation firm. Hiring employees for the project means that these individuals are paid directly by the customer. The right ones can manage the strategic project effectively and look out for the company's best interest. The downside is that, unless many of these implementations are executed and maintain an in-house implementation capability, the company might need to hire and fire, which reduces the pool of people who might want to work for the company due to the reputation of how employees are treated. In addition, it increases the cost. For this reason there are firms that provide this service.

2. Engage an intermediary organization to manage the implementation.

   These consultants are not responsible for the end-to-end performance of an implementation. Instead, their purpose is to advise a customer in the oversight of large implementations. A benefit of this approach is that this organization is charged with acting in the company's best interest. This company potentially will not be conflicted with the sometimes-competing goals of the implementation firm, while still having the necessary skills required to implement a complex program.

3. Trust the company's vendor management organization.

This is the path many organizations follow for an average-sized implementation. In this model, the company's vendor management organization (or procurement organization) creates a contract with penalties and rewards, metrics, and service-level agreements (SLAs) to create a balance between the vendor and the customer. Additionally, vendor management actually holds the vendor accountable for implementation details (e.g., dates and quality) rather than merely setting up the contract and walking away. In many cases, contracts are silent on specific roles, responsibilities, and SLAs. This is a potential problem to watch for. If this strategy is followed, the organization should have a very mature vendor management function.

1.7   Summary

The IT leaders who launch a project with a sharply focused plan, clear guidelines, and well-chosen support are the ones best equipped to shepherd a major IT project to its successful conclusion. The rewards of a successfully executed IT project can be tremendous.

In this section, customers of implementation firms learned what it takes to keep a project from falling into the litigation trap. The majority of the remainder of this is focused on strategizing for those projects that unfortunately have found themselves in court.

Expect the best, plan for the worst,
and prepare to be surprised.

—Denis Waitley

Section 2
Preparing for and Protecting Yourself in Litigation

In the systems implementation context, plan for the eventuality that the engagement will end up in litigation. If project leaders, from either an implementation firm or a customer of an implementation firm, plan as if the project will end up in litigation, the chances of sending that one email in the heat of the moment or regretting not thoroughly reviewing a set of deliverables are reduced.

So what does this mean tactically?

1. Assume EVERYTHING is legally discoverable. In other words, every document, internal or external, that pertains to this engagement or

this customer, even text messages, could end up in court. Yes, even that confidential sales document marked "for internal use only." Even the internal email, sent at 2 A.M. that says "Jimmy Bob Harddrive is a moron."

2. Remember what former Governor Spitzer said while he was attorney general of New York: *Never talk when you can nod and never nod when you can wink and never write an email, because it's death. You're giving prosecutors all the evidence we need.*

3. Sign-offs are important. These protect both parties and show agreement on timing and deliverables

4. Try and stay away from conjecture. As previously recognized, technology implementations are almost as much art as science; there are several ways to accomplish the goal, many of equal merit. Document key decision points, make sure the customer and the implementer agree, and move on.

5. When in doubt, over-document. This is particularly hard when it comes to Agile engagements, which are explained in more detail in Section 3.1.2, "The Systems Development Lifecycle (SDLC) and Methodologies," on page 58.

While technologists love to hate documentation, sometimes a single document can make all the difference in litigation.

6. Follow a consistent standard methodology. The most well-known methodologies are: LEAN, Agile, and Waterfall. Efficient or inefficient, stick with a consistent methodology and consistent deliverables.

7. Follow a consistent data preservation regimen that applies to all team members who touch the implementation project. Collect documents at the end, or during, an engagement in a consistent format, and preserve these items. Litigation sometimes happens years after the conclusion of the engagement.

2.1 Everything is Discoverable

If you take nothing else away from this section, this is the one thing to remember. It matters not if the email or presentation is marked "internal use only." It matters not if it was an internal discussion, insulting all of your customers equally. In what context something was said or someone wrote something doesn't make a difference; if it discusses the implementation firm's competition or decisions leading up to the engagement, assume it will ALL end up in court. Today, data is forever. Deleting

an email or a social media post does not necessarily
delete it from the server or the back-up or the cloud.
Assume all data is available forever.

2.2 Engagement Deliverables

Knowing that deliverables will be seen by the customer,
and possibly a jury, engagement deliverables should
be full of facts, not conjecture. Additionally, systems
implementers are wise to share draft deliverables
with customers well before their due date. This helps
in obtaining customer buy-in to the engagement
deliverable, making execution easier, especially if the
message being shared might be contentious.

2.3 Sign-offs

A sign-off is what it sounds like. The customer
or owner signs off, or agrees, to the deliverable.
Most key deliverables should be signed off: design
specifications, test plan items, and so on. Many
systems implementation contracts have an implied
sign-off, such as "five days after receipt, a deliverable is
considered signed off." This is not unreasonable most
of the time, but when an implementation goes into
litigation, it is much more helpful to have an actual
sign-off from the customer.

Try not to rely on verbal confirmation from the
customer; memories fade over time. An email that

states, "I have reviewed and accepted this deliverable" is around forever.

2.4 Requirements and Traceability

Communications around the design of the system are most often the source of disconnect between the implementer and customer, as highlighted by this cartoon from the 1970s.

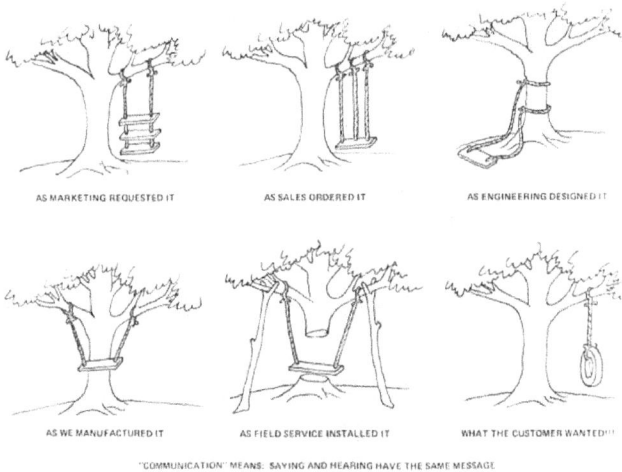

Figure 1—1970s Requirements Communication Cartoon (original author unknown, public domain)

Traceability is the ability to track the business or systems requirements as designed through testing to delivery. For example, looking at the tree swing in the cartoon, the requirements related to the tire (e.g., size) would be a set of requirements that we could trace into a test case (i.e., is the tire black and 18 inches tall?), which could be identified in production (tire model number XYZ).

All levels of requirements should be traceable, vetted, and signed off. Many times, only the highest level system requirements are vetted, ignoring the detailed or technical requirements. It is important to obtain validation of the lower-level and the top-level requirements.

Although the cartoon was created for humorous purposes, there is a great amount of truth to this illustration. We have all seen (or experienced) the miscommunication illustrated in the tree swing cartoon. Sign-offs prevent the disconnects that are commonplace between design and implementation, while proper traceability allows for the forensic connection to uncover who started the project on the wrong path. It may also provide an opportunity to alter course before litigation occurs.

2.5 Document, Document, Document

A 2005 adaptation of the previous tree swing cartoon adds a frame for "as we documented it," which is depicted as an empty field. It is common in large implementations to find gaps in documentation.

Agile methodologies are defined later in section 3.1.2, "The Systems Development Lifecycle (SDLC) and Methodologies," page 45. The relevancy here related to Agile development documentation is that some of the more spartan examples of systems documentation come out of Agile models. One method that is popular to combat this is to dedicate a scrum sprint, a set of Agile iterations, toward documentation. This has obvious drawbacks, but from what I have seen, this seems to work if documentation and Agile are important.

Important Types of Systems Documentation:

1. Blueprints and design specs (functional and technical requirements)

2. Test cycles, cases, and results

3. Traceability matrices

4. Program plans

5. Status reports

6. Change requests

7. Systems maintenance and support documentation

When documenting, however, do not forget the primary rule: assume everything is discoverable. I cannot tell you how many times I have done a post-implementation review of someone's code, and in the innards, there is some incriminating comment talking about "the guy who designed this business rule is an idiot." It seems harmless at the time. Who's ever going to look at code comments, right?

2.6 Methodology

This will not be a discussion about the pros and cons of various methodologies. For an overview see Section 3.1.7, "Key Acronyms and Terms," page 79. The key point about a methodology with respect to litigation is that the decisions on what the methodology will be and what the artifacts will look like should be made up front and adhered to.

Additionally, try not to combine multiple methods, meaning one should resist the urge to use traditional/waterfall and Agile together. Agree on the notations, diagrams, error handling, and exception criteria from the start. Pick a methodology, and stick with it where possible.

There are large benefits in methodology to large implementations. Consider this in the overall methodology plan, and try not to have documentation for documentation's sake.

2.7 Data Preservation

Data preservation rules vary, and differing industries and companies have differing regulations and policies around data retention. A company should preserve data on an ongoing basis or decide to dedicate time after their engagements to move all engagement documentation to a central repository.

I have seen two successful methods in preserving implementation-related documentation:

1. Collect documentation throughout the lifecycle of the engagement. Keep a running "binder" of critical documentation and deliverables.

2. In the month or so after an engagement completion (or completion of a significant phase), spend time to ensure all relevant documentation is placed in the correct location.

Have a person not connected with the engagement review the documentation for completeness.

Documentation is a large investment of time, but the potential savings are incalculable. It might seem like spending a thousand hours on one case a year is cheaper than using one hundred hours for every implementation to build these repositories, and if you are never served with a discovery request, this may be true. But if you do get one, you will find that nothing beats being prepared.

2.8 Specific Nuances for Implementers

The preceding paragraphs are applicable to implementers and customers alike, but there are a few areas that are specific to just implementers.

1. Document Resourcing Decisions—Document and share with the customer the proposed team members and their experience levels.

2. Key Personnel—For any shifts made to key personnel, get the customer involved as soon as possible and document their involvement. If it is appropriate, consult them during the replacement decision process.

3. Customer Initiated Personnel Change—If this happens, the customer should be included in replacement personnel decisions.

FEES

Don't bill the customer more than agreed.

Errors happen. These need to be fixed, documented, and processed without delay. Also, try not to be shy about showing where value was added beyond what the customer asked for. Likewise, don't be shy to take credit for what was done well, and be open to feedback on where improvements could be made.

Bottom line: accept responsibility for errors and don't be shy about communicating the value delivered.

CHANGE REQUESTS

Change requests are an important area of analysis in systems implementations. There should be a formal change request process with integrated sign-offs, and the implementer must be diligent about what change requests are accepted.

Additionally, as a part of the change management governance process, change requests should be analyzed against their original requirements for ripple effects from these changes in design, implementation, and support. Changes that do have wide-reaching effects should be broadly communicated to all affected parties.

2.9 Specific Nuances for Customers of Implementers

There are a few considerations that are specific for the customers of implementers.

VENDOR MANAGEMENT

Vendor management organizations vary in maturity. Oftentimes, the vendor management group within the company negotiates contracts that have service-level agreements (SLAs) that are not monitored over the life of the project. In some cases, however, vendor management will monitor SLAs and vendor performance, and they may help negotiate if concessions are warranted.

The highly mature vendor management organization might be able to help prevent issues with:

a. collecting data on the vendor related to other programs

b. performance metrics

c. accurate billing information

d. determining if the implementer lived up to contract demands

DOCUMENT GRIEVANCES

In some cases the implementation firms are unaware of a problem—if they don't know, they can't fix it. Documenting any issues is important. In many cases, when issues are documented in a thoughtful and methodical way, the results may be surprising.

Computers are like Old Testament gods;
lots of rules and no mercy.

—Joseph Campbell

Section 3
For Lawyers
Representing Litigants in
Implementation Matters

This section is primarily for those attorneys with clients facing litigation. In this section, the terminology that technology experts will use, key concepts about a systems implementation dispute, and the attributes that are important for finding a systems implementation expert will be described.

First, a bit about the potential clients in this area:

- A systems implementation firm

- The customer of an implementation firm

- Users or recipients of benefits from the system, not directly linked to the implementer or the customer of the implementer.

Most commonly, implementation firms end up as defendants as they are reluctant to bring suit against their customers. Therefore, most of this section will be geared toward defending an implementation firm. Aspects of representing an implementation firm as a plaintiff will also be touched upon.

3.1 Technology Primer for Attorneys

If you are like most attorneys, you aren't paid to know the idiosyncrasies of technology any more than I should know the differences between torts or constitutional law. Yet when working with a technology implementation firm, you will need to be conversant in the basics of technology.

It is a commonly held belief that some computer systems are more complicated to understand and operate than the space shuttle, and they are viewed as the most complicated things humans have yet developed. I bring this up because I in no way am trying to dumb down systems implementations, or make them seem easy. They are anything but.

Systems implementations can be extremely complicated, which is why many of these implementations cost hundreds of millions of dollars, take multiple years, and require the help of hundreds of highly trained and skilled people, just for a single implementation. This is merely mentioned as the following topics are just the basics so that you may understand technology implementation clients a little better

3.1.1 COTS vs. Custom

Many implementations start with the customization of a commercial off-the-shelf (COTS) product. Implementations can also involve completely customized software (which typically is more expensive) and, in rare cases, uncustomized software (which is typically the least expensive option).

It is interesting to note that some of the largest *custom* systems implementers are also some of the largest implementers of COTS systems. There are many reasons for this:

a. The skillset required to customize a piece of software is often similar to the skill required to build from scratch.

b. The more customization required, the higher the complexity, and the rarer the skill.

c. It is rare that a small implementation firm will be able to field a bench large enough

> to customize large efforts; many of these
> efforts have hundreds of individuals
> deployed, which leads to larger firms.

COTS

Simplistically speaking, customized commercial off-
the-shelf (COTS) software works like Microsoft Excel.
When a new, blank spreadsheet is opened, it doesn't do a
thing. However, the power behind Excel is tremendous
when it is told what to do. Likewise, with these super-
large COTS customizations, there is basically a system
teeming with configuration options, which are virtually
limitless but essentially powerless until told what to do.

Enterprise Resource Planning (ERP) is one of
the major categories of COTS systems. There are
major implementation firms in each space within the
industry that cater to large implementations in specific
industry categories. The most well-known in this
category are SAP and Oracle. These firms are typically
associated with expensive software, highly specialized
resource requirements, and long implementation
timeframes.

If it is expensive, time-consuming, and difficult
to find any resources, why does anyone go the route
of customized COTS? The answer is pretty simple:
Configuring a solution is usually faster, cheaper, less
complex, and less risky than starting from scratch.

The following diagram demonstrates the relationship between a customer's system requirements and what a typical COTS solution offers.

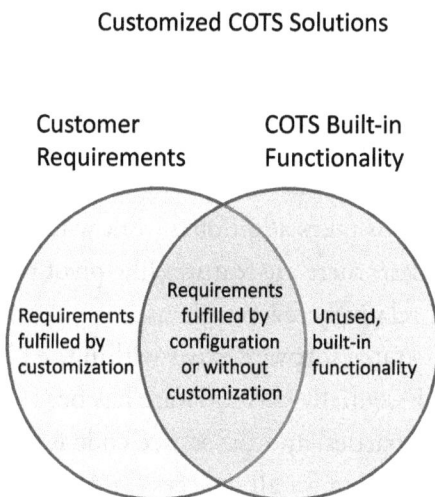

Customized COTS Solutions

Customer Requirements   COTS Built-in Functionality

Requirements fulfilled by customization

Requirements fulfilled by configuration or without customization

Unused, built-in functionality

Figure 2—Requirements Met by COTS Software

Typically, there is a subset of functionality that meets requirements ready out-of-the-box, or through minor configuration. This is represented in the middle. When required functionality does not come readily from the package, customization or additional tools are necessary for the software to function as intended. This is depicted on the left. Interestingly, in any COTS package, the base platform contains pre-existing features that may not be needed, which is essentially functionality that is being paid for but not used, as depicted on the right.

To describe the above diagram using an everyday example: in Microsoft Excel, out-of-the-box software does calculation, sorting, filtering, and more. It only takes some minor input and configurations to perform such functions, which fits most user requirements. However, a customer might need to sort through massive amounts of data and connect to an external data store. This takes additional work with another database. Last, there are features like pivot tables in Excel that relatively few people use.

Open-source software exists within the COTS umbrella. Essentially this software has been developed by multiple parties, and the source code is placed into the public domain for all to access and use for free.

While much of the software in implementation disputes is not open-source (also known as proprietary), the use of open-source is gaining traction. This makes for unique quandaries considering liability.

Additionally, since COTS solutions have a broader user base, are competitive, and may be subjected to regulatory scrutiny, they typically conform to a set of development standards. This is especially important when regulations around data protection and privacy are considered, because encryption and authentication features within a COTS system are typically robust.

As stated earlier, this is the type of systems implementation most companies embark on today. They purchase a COTS product and customize it to meet their requirements. The art of this is to pick the product that allows the customer to meet their requirements with minimal alterations, without having to pay for features they will never use.

Custom Development

Custom development has become rarer as time goes on, because vendors have entered the space to fulfill these needs, including more traditional "custom" vendors that have developed adaptable products themselves. Assuming the initiatives are large enough to be a candidate for litigation, they usually involve implementation timeframes of years.

Ironically, the implementation skill requirements for custom development are often less onerous than some of the COTS options. I say this because there are simply more people who know basic coding languages than proprietary systems. Additionally, individuals with little experience or directly out of school are likely to know a few basic languages but might have little familiarity with systems produced by SAP and Oracle.

The following diagram is intended to show the stark contrast between a customized COTS solution and a custom solution.

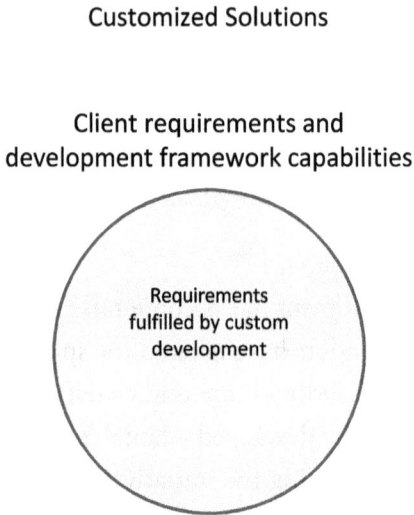

Customized Solutions

Client requirements and development framework capabilities

Requirements fulfilled by custom development

Figure 3—Requirements Met by Custom Software

A custom solution ideally meets all the customer's requirements. No requirements go unmet, and the system doesn't perform unnecessary functionality. It's like the difference between an off-the-rack and custom suit. The custom suit fits you almost perfectly, doesn't use any extra material that you don't need, but likely won't fit anyone else as well.

3.1.2 THE SYSTEMS DEVELOPMENT LIFECYCLE (SDLC) AND METHODOLOGIES

The methodology leveraged in the implementation will likely help determine the phasing that the implementation project will undergo. While there are many deviations in nomenclature, the largest common similarities in phases are as follows.

Plan

The planning phase is the phase where the initial project scope is set, milestones established, and high-level work plans are created. The teams are identified in this phase, and high-level cost and effort estimates are created. It is important to note that not every project has a plan phase, but there is a direct correlation between project complexity and the importance of performing a planning phase.

Design

The software doesn't do anything until it is told what to do. This is the phase when someone tells the system how to function. Typically, the customer explains to the implementer what the system is being designed for, and the implementer documents these requirements, which will be addressed in the next phase.

A common phrase for this is "two in a box." This means a business analyst and a technologist sit down and design (and in Agile methodologies, they build and test together). Sometimes the planning phase is combined with the design phase.

Design is a critical phase of systems development. If no one tells the system what to do, it likely won't function in the way it is desired. It's really that simple.

Key Point: Generally, in a COTS implementation, the system is customized somewhere in the 20 percent range, as the remaining 80 percent is common among differing customers with minor configurations making up the bulk of the implementations. This customized 20 percent is usually the hardest part.

Build

The build phase usually entails the bulk of the effort. Basically, the system is coded/configured or otherwise told what to do during the build. This is where all the specialized skills come into play. Often, this phase, called "unit testing," is actually considered in the build phase. Essentially, this is where the developer "bench tests" their code individually at a high level to see if it meets the needs of the design.

Test
The test phase is also called quality assurance, or "QA," and it is during this phase that the system components are tested to determine whether or not they meet documented requirements. The major test phases can be subdivided into:

- Unit Test—This test phase is usually considered a portion of "Build," but it is important to note here. This is the first test phase where a developer begins to test the code.

- String Test—Several modules are strung together to ensure messages are passed correctly and that they work together as designed. This test is performed by developers.

- System Test—This is the first time the system is assembled together as a cohesive set and tested from end to end. Consequently, this is often the first time major issues begin to appear. In some cases, the testing team is made up of designers and developers.

- Performance Test—This is where the system is tested to see whether or not it meets the speed, throughput, and/or processing requirements. It is made up of subphases such as load/stress testing, which tell us how the system behaves when everything is thrown at it.

- User Acceptance Test (UAT)—This is a very important yet often underutilized test. In UAT the user community, sometimes composed of former designers and/or end users, test the system. They typically use system test scripts with extended data and real-life scenarios to determine whether or not it meets the requirements and "accepts" the system.

This may be underutilized in troubled implementations because the overall testing phase is being squeezed due to budget constraints. When this happens, UAT is looked upon as a luxury. That means that UAT, rather than being treated as the important test stream that it is, becomes another system test cycle or is overlooked altogether.

A customary practice is to use a Requirements Verification List (RVL), which is signed off by the customer when acceptance criteria are met. This is a list of major requirements that have been validated and witnessed by the customer through UAT. This is a way to audit an implementation to ensure the product is delivered as promised.

Deploy

In the deploy, or rollout, phase, features, applications, and systems are rolled out into production, also called "go-live." This phase is sometimes followed by phases known as deployment support or continuous improvement. These post-deployment phases involve supporting the customer in performing fixes, additional training, or subsequent additional releases to support or improve upon the original implementation. The period of production support can range from months to years, depending on the system's complexity or other desires of the customer.

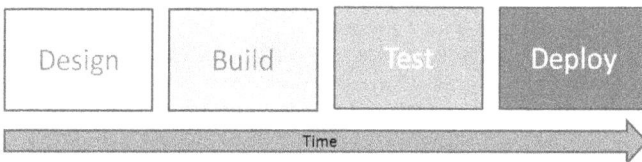

Figure 4—Typical SDLC Phases

3.1.3 REQUIREMENTS

Throughout the book, I have used the word *requirements* rather loosely. Requirements are the specifications of what the system that has been developed is meant to perform. Plainly speaking, it is what the system is supposed to do. It is an agreement between those that understand the business functions to be performed and those that will engineer the system to perform those functions. There are quite a few different types of requirements:

Table 3—Types of Requirements

Requirements Category	Description
System-Level Requirements	Define the overall parameters, objectives, and scope of the system at large. For instance: "The billing system will create invoices for all current customers in Ohio."
Functional Requirements	These requirements are the next level down. They break the system requirements to a level from which process, design documentation, and ultimately code can be derived. This is the *what* of what a system does. For example: "The system will create an invoice for all vehicle orders in the current calendar month on the last day of every month." (Additional requirements might detail what data is invoiced, who reviews, who approves, etc.)
Nonfunctional Requirements (aka Technical Requirements)	These detail the *how* and *how many* for the functional requirement. An example: "The system will process a maximum of two thousand invoices a month, and the data will be retained on the system for a period of seven years."

3.1.4 SIGN-OFFS

Getting a customer's sign-off is an important area within large-scale implementations. This can be done electronically, either through an email or through the system that tracks approvals. Of course, actual signatures can be captured.

Major artifacts that are often subject to sign-off in a large-scale implementation include:

1. Project Charter—Documents the project's scope, approach, key dates, budgets, resources, deliverables, objectives, and risks

2. Functional Requirements/Specifications—The *what* a system is intended to do

3. Technical Requirements/Specification—The *how* or *how many times* the system is to perform the function

4. Test Cycles/Plans—The various phases and types of tests the system undergoes

5. Test Results—The documented results of the various test phases

6. Project Plans—The plans, or Work Breakdown Structures (WBS), for the project.

If sign-offs are not obtained, it leaves the question of customer approval uncertain. However, most implementation contracts routinely state that deliverables are "automatically" accepted after a period of a few days.

Table 4—Commonly signed-off artifacts

Deliverable	Typical Responsible Signer	Key Point
Functional requirements	Functional design lead and project sponsor	Are requirements verifiable/testable, concise, traceable, consistent, complete, and necessary?
Technical requirements	Technical design lead and project sponsor	Are requirements verifiable/testable, concise, traceable, consistent, complete, and necessary?
Test cycles/ plans	Test lead, design lead, and program sponsor	Are all requirements tested, including negative conditions?
Test results	Test lead, design lead, and program sponsor	Do the test results prove the system will meet requirements?
Program plans	All leads, PMO, and project sponsor	Are timelines consistent and achievable? Are parties notified of changes?

3.1.5 RELEASE PHASING

Most projects are implemented in multiple releases of software, not to be confused with SDLC phasing highlighted above. The phases may correspond to varying groups of functionality, geographic areas, or user communities.

The opposite of delivery in phases is called the big-bang method. This was popular when everything was on a mainframe and everyone was connected to a singular, central system. As mentioned previously, big-bang implementations are risky and typically have higher failure rates.

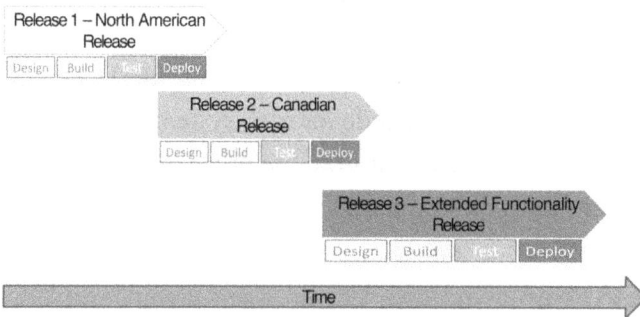

Figure 5—Example of Phased Implementation Approach

3.1.6 ARCHITECTURAL COMPONENTS

Entire books—no, entire series of books—have been dedicated to systems architecture principles. The following are distilled categories many attorneys think are important.

Infrastructure

This is the basic component of computer systems; it is the tangible part of an implementation; the parts that can be touched (even if they are all in the cloud). Simplistically, one can think of it as the "hardware": wires, boxes, fiber optic networks, routers, switches, and servers.

Middleware

The layer of software/hardware appliances that act as a buffer between interfacing systems, the middleware is essentially a translator between systems. In the early days of computing, point-to-point interfaces were made, pieces of code for each system to talk to each other directly. With the use of middleware, each system can talk to the middleware layer instead.

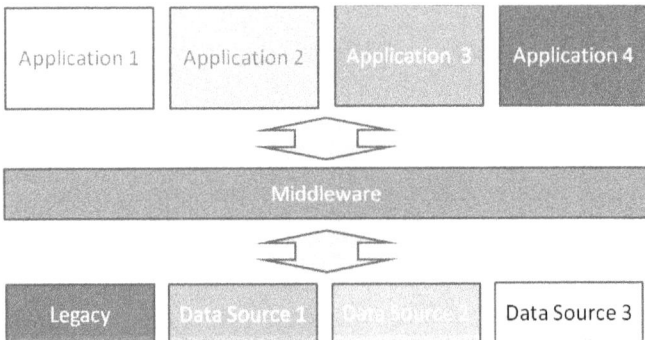

Figure 6—Interface Development Utilizing Middleware

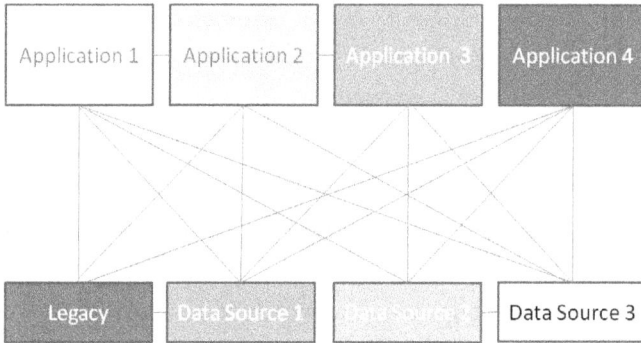

Figure 7—Interface Development without Middleware

End-user Systems

The interface of the system the user actually interacts with, end-user systems, get the most attention. This system is usually a small subset of the implementation, but being that it is the potion people interact with, it is what customers often respond to.

Mainframes, Legacy Systems, and Host

A mainframe is a very large computer sitting on a raised floor in a largely empty room. It is the center or hub of all the systems' actions in many companies, and it is literally running hundreds of applications at the same time. Many organizations have stated goals to move away from mainframes, but since this is where most of the organization's business rules are, as well as where most of the organizational data and processing occurs, this is a very difficult goal.

Workflow, Business Process Management (BPM), and Business Rules Engines (BRE)

Essentially these are systems that automate the process that is performed by systems or individuals. These are classified by different languages and are sometimes categorized with middleware. While these components are not an absolute requirement in implementations, they are gaining in popularity largely due to the productivity enhancements gained by their use. These systems can speed, automate, and track processes that are performed.

Data

This refers to the data that is required for the system. There are series of books that are dedicated to this topic. Some of the high-level concepts are:

Table 5—High-Level Data Concepts Important for Litigation

High Level Data Concept	Description	Key Point
Structured data	The time-honored standard database, rows and tables, or cubes	Legacy systems are typically this type, sometimes subject to data manipulation, extraction, or transformation
Unstructured data	Data not in a database—for instance, this manuscript. Typically, some kind of extraction needs to be performed to use this as data, or use a tool that works with unstructured datasets	Traditionally, this was a thorny problem for organizations to solve, but with the adoption of many newer tools, this is less an issue today

High Level Data Concept	Description	Key Point
Data warehouse	A centralized store of data	There are sometimes entire projects devoted to building data warehouses
Data lake	A data warehouse that is not full of completely normalized data; specialized tools can comb though the data to obtain desired results	A relatively newer concept that is gaining traction

3.1.7 KEY ACRONYMS AND TERMS

This entire book could be on acronyms and key terms, but let's discuss the most important of those you will encounter and need to make sense of:

Deliverables

Deliverables are items produced out of a process. For instance, an item produced out of the planning process is a Work Breakdown Structure (WBS), out of design, a requirements document. Deliverables can be anything tangible written down, (also referred to as artifacts); they can be documents, spreadsheets, code, and so on.

RICEF

Common in enterprise resource planning (ERP) engagements, this is the development effort around reports, interfaces, conversions, enhancements, and forms (RICEF).

- Reports—One of the key systems outputs of the system, these can include inventory reports, month-end profitability reports, etc.

- Interfaces—Key system interfaces connect to external systems, legacy data, etc.

- Conversion—A conversion object is a module that takes data from an external system and converts it into a format that the core system can understand.

- Enhancement—Usually this is an exit out of the core ERP system. It will be related to a function that the core system cannot handle, or the implementation requires a proprietary piece of functionality.

- Forms—These are specific scripts and modules that are highlighted for printing. Like reports, there are specific commands required for building these (e.g., smartforms, scripts).

Functional and Technical Design

They are also called specifications or requirements. The functional side is the recipe for *what* the system is to do (e.g., criteria and steps for a loan approval). The technical side is *how* and/or *how many times* the functional side is done (e.g., how often loan approvals are expected to be requested). Collectively these make up *systems requirements*.

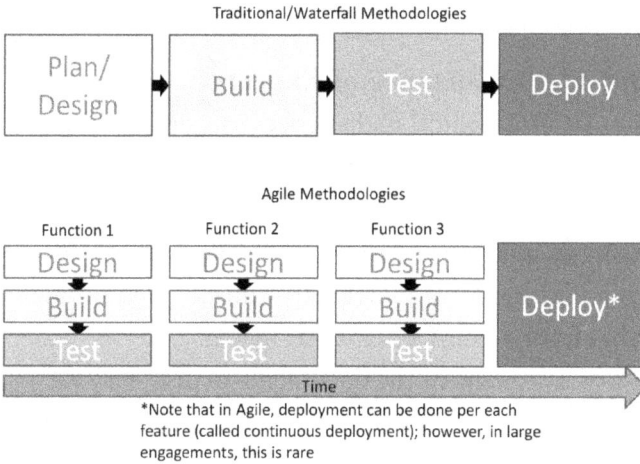

Traditional/Waterfall Methodologies

Plan/Design → Build → Test → Deploy

Agile Methodologies

Function 1: Design → Build → Test
Function 2: Design → Build → Test
Function 3: Design → Build → Test
Deploy*

Time

*Note that in Agile, deployment can be done per each feature (called continuous deployment); however, in large engagements, this is rare

Figure 8—Traditional/Waterfall Methods vs. Agile

Methodologiest

There are many differing methods used to implement projects, and some of these differences are not trivial. Entire series of books are devoted to the various methodologies, so I cannot fully do them justice here. Therefore, to simplify, there are two major camps: Traditional/Waterfall and Agile.

In general, Waterfall goes from design to build to test in distinct phases. One comes after the other, and the work flows from one stage to the next. In Agile, the three major phases are performed together. A paired team of designer and developer designs, builds, and tests a module or application before going to the next.

3.2 The Importance of Experts

Similar to a medical malpractice case, no amount of studying is going to make an attorney a doctor. No matter how thorough a book this may be, it will not make an attorney a systems expert. For this reason, you need a team of individuals who can look through what transpired in a particular matter.

While many of the documents in discovery are redundant or superfluous, you can leverage a group of experts to determine what is important, what is not, and ultimately conclude what transpired throughout these long journeys from design to build to final delivery.

An expert can help in a number of ways:

1. Before a litigation decision is made:
   Does the client have a case? In a matter of weeks, a team of experts can help determine the high-level positives and negatives of the case, including where potential weaknesses lie. If there is a well-informed idea on the relative

strength of the case, you can invest litigation dollars more wisely.

2. In discovery:

An interesting nuance in systems implementation matters are versions of critical documents. It is common to have a "final" deliverable, but in discovery, were prior versions of these documents included? Which of these are really important? It is also common to have documents embedded in other documents, and these are not always provided during discovery. Unfortunately, it is not as simple as "the latest version is the best" as what changes from version to version may be critical.

3. In depositions:

A truly expert systems implementation team can inform the legal team on areas to examine for in deposition. This includes identifying key documents and key topics for cross-examination.

4. In trial:

As in typical commercial litigation, experts can provide opinions at trial. There is little variation from other types of experts, but this will be covered later in this section.

5. In working with the client:

> You know this better than I: clients are usually not impartial about the role they played in the matter. A third party, whose role it is to get to the truth no matter what it is, can provide feedback in working with the client to potentially seek to adjust expectations.

The earlier an expert is brought on board, the easier it will be to navigate these difficult cases.

3.4 Interacting with Systems Experts

Experts are common in commercial litigation, and as attorneys you usually interact with the legal team and experts by phone and in person. If potential systems implementation experts are not familiar with a verbal communication style, it is important to have a conversation with the team to set up expectations for future communications.

During the first meeting with the expert team, you might need to get on the same page regarding how you will stay in regular contact with each other during the course of the engagement.

3.5 Discovery Is Not Just about Documents

We are in an era where many deliverables subject to discovery were never documents to begin with.

This is especially critical in systems implementation litigation. Proper assessment of these items typically requires special tools and skills. Many crucial items are easily missed in discovery requests.

Metadata

Metadata is technically "data about data." This is how we describe a set of data, which could include the file author, dates created and modified, file sizing, location, owner, and other traceability information. This is important in this field for many reasons, including version control for files as well as authorship/ownership.

So how is the original metadata obtained?

The easiest way is to preserve the repository. Documents are typically stored in Microsoft SharePoint or some other document storage tool, but routinely, when a discovery request is put in place, it may only address the documents, not the metadata or repository.

Key Point: There are commands to export metadata from most storage repositories. If it is feasible, getting the metadata will make your job, and that of your experts, much easier.

Databases

Several types of databases are put in use within an implementation project:

1. Databases that are part of the deliverables of the engagement (e.g., marketing, conversion, and customer)

2. Databases put in place for the management of the project.

Common databases that are used for the management of the project are:

1. Data that supports the project management function, including issues logs and risks logs

2. Data that supports the schedule, including project plan, budgeting, and resource spend/ utilization

3. Data that supports the implementation, including processes, requirements, test scripts, and test data

Few of these items are likely to be well-represented by a single document. In some cases, like an issues log contained within Microsoft SharePoint, they do not exist as a document at all and will likely not be within the production by default. In these cases, an extract of the database will be the most efficient way in which these items can be examined.

Code
Code is the software being developed by the implementer to deliver to the customer. This could be in a myriad of proprietary languages and is usually counted in the millions of lines in large engagements.

Version Control Software
Version control software is the mechanism to control and manage changes to code or other deliverables over time. These consist of databases of code, deliverables, and metadata. Version control software keeps track and documents changes to these deliverables as changes are made. These repositories usually reside within applications like PVCS, ClearCase, and SourceSafe.

Ancillary Systems
Last, in large implementations, there are supporting systems that are used solely for the implementation itself or that become a permanent part of the infrastructure. These applications can be for requirements management, test management, and trouble ticket tracking, to name a few. The figures below summarize these ancillary systems.

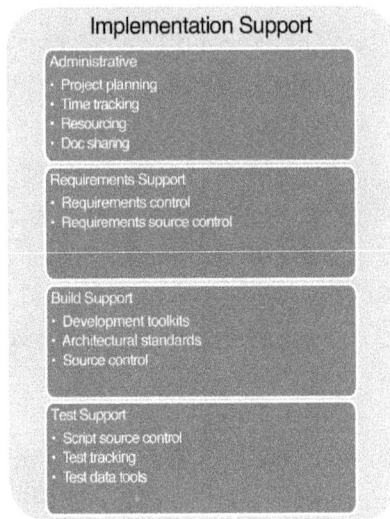

Figure 9.1—Examples of Ancillary Systems

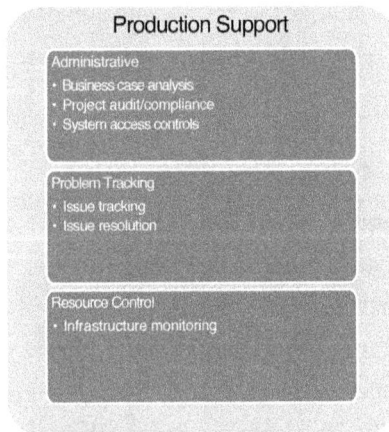

Figure 9.2—Examples of Ancillary Systems

From then on, when anything went wrong with a computer, we said it had bugs in it.

—Grace Hopper

Section 4

Further Litigation Expertise Related to Systems Disputes

This section is intended to discuss other areas of expertise that might be required in a system implementation matter and highlights more specific areas as it relates to expert selection.

This section is relevant for both implementation firms and customers of implementation firms.

4.1 Damages and Valuation

A key area where systems implementation expertise is required relates to evaluating damages. This is likely more similar to other experts you have consulted, as it is more of an accounting exercise than a systems-related skill. They will need to understand the components of the system in question and how that affects the damages model.

What follows are key areas for valuation of damages in a systems implementation matter.

COST OF THE IMPLEMENTATION SERVICES

This is expressed as the value of the services performed by individuals deployed to the implementation. This could include the implementation firm, other contractors utilized in the implementation, the customer resources used (either directly or indirectly), project management, and executive time spent on the implementation.

COST OF THE IMPLEMENTATION SOFTWARE

This is the total cost of software tools used during the implementation, such as the core software and any supporting tools. This includes project management tools, design aids, and testing aids as well as any additional tools that support the core system, like reporting software, middleware, database software, and analytical tools.

HARDWARE COSTS

Costs related to hardware utilized for the implementation should include development, test, and production hardware. This also includes shared resources such as network, mainframe, servers, and help desk.

BUSINESS CASE BENEFIT (OR COST) MEASUREMENT

There is a reason an implementation occurred, a business case somewhere that drove the investment. As such, if there was a delay in delivery, or if something did not get built as planned, there will likely be a delay damages.

COMPLIANCE COSTS

In some cases, implementations are driven from a compliance requirement. If there is a delay, or if any items were not delivered as expected, there might be costs associated with noncompliance.

THIRD-PARTY COSTS

There might be damages claims from your clients' customers—for example, inaccurate reports or delays in shipping items. These costs may be based on unpaid invoices or a delay in benefit receipt.

SOFT COSTS

This can include reputation damage, goodwill impairments, loss of trading partners, loss of access to certain markets, or loss of market share to competitors.

These are examples of areas where a damages expert who is adequately experienced in systems implementation can assist in the creation of a damages model.

4.2 Liability as It Relates to Timing

Timing is another area of expertise that may be a part of liability or damages. The delay may be such a large component that it needs to be assessed separately.

DELAY CAUSATION

This is the determination of why the delay occurred. Typically, this is a large portion of the liability expert's assessment. But the linkage between the liability expert and the damages expert cannot be ignored. Depending on the findings from the liability witness, certain factors and costs may or may not be pertinent. Sometimes this type of assessment can be performed without a broader liability witness program.

Computer science is no more about computers
than astronomy is about telescopes.

— Edsger Dijkstra

Section 5
Other System-Related
Areas of Litigation

This section is intended to briefly discuss other topics that are indirectly related to systems implementation matters. Some relate particularly to large-scale implementations.

5.1 Intellectual Property Disputes

These matters may be similar to other intellectual property (IP) disputes. In some instances, the implementation firm has created intellectual property out of work done for their customer, and they seek to protect it and put various restrictions on their customer's use of that IP; especially when an implementation firm is replaced during the course of an implementation project, IP-related issues might emerge.

SOFTWARE IP DISPUTES

These disputes could center on a software system's features, use of proprietary code or languages, or proprietary security/encryption protocols.

HARDWARE IP DISPUTES

These disputes could relate to a hardware system's features, use of proprietary chipsets, or proprietary storage technology.

PROCESS/METHOD OR OTHER PROPRIETARY TRADE MATTERS

There are specific IP concerns that relate to processes and methodologies that are utilized in the creation of a software or hardware product. These types of disputes are rare.

TRADEMARK/PATENT

Just like any other good or service, unique software and hardware features and products are widely protected via patent law.

5.2 Software/Warranty

These are relatively common disputes with large implementations. COTS software usually comes with some type of very limited warranty, which is enumerated in an end-user license agreement (EULA). The reason these end up in dispute is sometimes the customers expect support to come "free." It is relatively uncommon for heavily customized or custom systems to come with a warranty when post-production support is typically an additional phase to the build of the system

One way that an implementation firm can avoid this scenario is to begin to discuss production support, including the fact that it is an additional service with a separate cost, at the outset of the program.

5.3 Hardware/Warranty

Given the decreasing costs associated with hardware, combined with the fact that hardware purchase contracts are relatively clear when it comes to warranty periods and what is covered, these disputes are relatively rare. However, disconnects can occur with data loss due to hardware failure. As the line between software and hardware becomes more blurred (e.g., "appliances" that used to be software) this picture is becoming more complicated. Additionally, through cyber security breaches, as well as the increasing amount of data that is being stored, the potential liability from these failures due to the related business loss is increasing.

5.4 Data/Security Breach

As we have seen with the security breaches at Home Depot, Target, and many health insurance companies including Blue Cross Blue Shield, data loss is likely the largest growing area of concern.

Security can be breached from the outside, "lost" by the data owner, stolen by malicious employees, or kidnapped through malicious code or through the inside or the outside in the course of transmission to a third party. Areas to examine for litigation:

1. Did the data holder and any responsible third parties maintain adequate, reasonable controls over the data?

    a. Access control and monitoring (who has access to what, and what can they do within the system)

    b. Physical access control and monitoring (who has physical access to the devices holding data)

    c. Data protections, including encryption

    d. Data backup and controls

    e. External access prevention/firewalls

f. Access to data by third parties, authorized and unauthorized

2. Did the data holder notify those affected by any breach in a timely manner?

    a. Remediation activities

    b. Specific notification of what data was accessed

    c. Potential activities those affected by the breach can take

3. What were the potential damages due to the breach?

Many government regulations are related to this area. Some of the more common ones are HIPAA, Sarbanes-Oxley (SOX), Gramm Leach, GLBA, GDPR, and Reg P. These regulations come from federal regulatory bodies, as well as state and local regulators.

5.5 Class Actions and Other Third-Party Implementation Disputes

While this book focuses on the common contractual dispute between an implementer and customers of implementers, there are avenues when third parties may get involved with systems implementation disputes. These sometimes result in class-action suits or other types of third-party claims:

END CUSTOMERS THAT EXPECT A SERVICE OR BENEFIT
Customers who either bought or otherwise relied on a good or service and were affected by a systems implementation have begun to make claims in this area. They are alleging impacts related to timing of the receipt of the good or service, its cost, or its quality.

SHAREHOLDERS
Shareholder suits are beginning to emerge that relate to systems implementations. The allegation looks as this: Because of this implementation's late completion, a) the stock price went down or b) the merger price was overvalued or c) the merger should never have happened as the value paid for systems assets were too high, etc.

OTHERS
This broad topic relates to parties that receive benefits that could have been delayed or incorrect due to systems limitations. This includes insurance claims, Medicare payments, and the like.

Computers are incredibly fast, accurate and stupid. Human beings are incredibly slow, inaccurate and brilliant. Together they are powerful beyond imagination.

– Albert Einstein

Section 6
Begin with the End in Mind

Sales and Contracting

How does any organization that desires a new software system know who to select as an implementer in the first place? The path chosen will likely dictate the destination, so choose the implementer with the end in mind. There are many tasks and responsibilities that occur in the sales, negotiation, and contracting phases that can positively or negatively influence a project's direction. To be fair, there are as many implementations that break all the rules that execute well as there are projects that have amazing contracting phases that go off the rails. However, the below best practices can reduce some of the heartburn that will naturally occur in any complex systems implementation.

Pre-Sales Overview

Before the implementation begins, there are a few key interactions that occur that influence the possible direction of any systems implementation.

These are the introductory or sales phase and the contracting phase. The sales phase may include a Request for Information (RFI) from the customer to narrow the field of implementers to only those that can meet specifications. Then the process should consist of a Request for Proposal (RFP) or some other document that solicits a proposal from an implementation firm. The proposal is usually accompanied by multiple meetings to tailor the engagement.

The other phase is the negotiation and contracting phase, which usually results in Master Services Agreements (MSA), Service Level Agreements (SLA), and Statements of Work (SOW).

As a general rule, if the implementer's sales team is difficult to communicate with to set meetings, nonresponsive, or generally appears to be spread too thin, this is an indication that this particular implementer might be running lean, and the rest of an implementation might present resourcing challenges.

The mantra: if the sales process is cumbersome, then the implementation might be troubled.

It can be tempting to choose the implementer with the long list of stellar clients and impressive resumes, but if communication is a struggle early on, communication might be a struggle throughout the project.

When it comes to negotiation, there does not to appear to be a correlation between how difficult the implementer's legal team is and implementation success.

There are examples of legal teams on both sides of the table with absolute bulldogs as well as generally cordial legal teams with success and failures in their history. However, there does appear to be a correlation with the overall implementer's organizational culture and the customer experience.

Culture is everything. If the implementation firm's internal counsel is rude or not customer centric it is quite possible to be a pervasive behavior rather than the exception. Culture affects attitude, deliverables, and whether or not a team will over- or underdeliver. Does integrity matter to the leaders of the organization? Understand a company's culture to understand if they are the right fit with yours.

While important, RFPs are typically not legally binding. This is because the scope or objective of the project will likely evolve between the RFP phase and the actual contract. Nevertheless, RFPs are oftentimes key documents in litigation.

It is relatively common for a sales team (and this even comes out in an RFP) to overpromise on their team's or the software capabilities. This is rarely caused by outright misrepresentation. This is typically caused by the deep layers of complexity in contemporary solutions, resulting in confusion at the sales and frequently the implementation firm's technical support level. For this reason, larger, more risky engagements should engage a third party to dig deeper, provide an impartial opinion, or otherwise assist in this process.

Negotiation
There are several key points related to negotiation that can reduce risk in an implementation.

Customer Side Deal Team
There should be professional vendor management personnel involved with contracting and the deal team. There can also be input from third parties who might be familiar with the implementation firm or the space. It is important to have another set of eyes involved in addition to the implementation firm and the individuals that will be managing the firm.

Timing: There is a correlation between the timing or difficulty of executing a contract and the difficulty in dealing with an implementation firm. It appears that the manufacturer that inordinately slows down a contract execution might suffer from widespread resource constraints, which may cause difficulty down the line.

Contracting

At a macro-level, there appears to be a correlation between organization and deal size, and who originates the contract (whose template is used, the implementation firm's or the customer's). Typically, this is weighted toward which organization is bigger with large engagements; in small engagements, it typically defaults to the implementation firm. There does not appear to be a correlation between failure and the origination party, but there is a correlation between failure and utilizing the implementation firm's boiler plate contract without modifications. In these cases of using a system implementation firm's default contract, there is typically a lack of clarity around key areas (detailed below).

There are a few main contracting types, each highlighted below with their areas of potential concern:

- Time and Materials (T&M): The simplest and still most common contracting type with implementations is Time and Materials. This basically means the customer will pay an agreed-upon rate times the amount of time it takes for completion, plus out of pocket expenses (i.e., software, travel, etc.). This contract type is the most flexible for both parties. With no set total contract price, a T&M contract often results in costs exceeding the original project's budget.

- Time and Materials with cap: A T&M contract with a cap on the total dollar amount. In my experience these are rare, as they give a benefit to a customer without any potential upside to the implementation firm.

- Fixed Fee: An agreed-upon price is negotiated, and that, in theory, is the price that is paid. These contract types are inflexible when it comes to scope changes. Minor change requests are usually accommodated, but when a large change in direction is encountered, the contracts should be renegotiated.

- Milestone-Based Contracts: In these contracts, the implementation firm is paid each time a certain milestone or deliverable is complete. These are effective contracts if they clearly define the milestones and the milestone-acceptance criteria. This contract type is also relatively inflexible for large scope changes. Milestone contracts based solely on dates do not typically work well.

- Incentive-based contracts: These were all the rage in the early 2000s but have fallen out of favor. The reason is that it is difficult to align the incentives with the desired behavior at the outset. It is difficult to obtain granular enough metrics related to the desired behavior. At the same time, the more granular and numerous the metrics are, the more difficult they are to monitor. Then, of course these contracts should be monitored at a detailed level, and that has a cost. There are examples of engagements where the implementation firm was paid 100 percent of all incentives yet resulted in litigation because the customer did not like the results of the implementation.

Specific Contract Provisions

One of the most important overall comments related to contracting is to be as specific as possible in the following key areas:

ROLES AND RESPONSIBILITIES:

It is important to define the specific roles and responsibilities of the implementer, and the customer, as well as any third parties within the contract. It is permissible to use individual names if appropriate. Pay special attention to project managers. There are likely multiple individuals fulfilling this role, and to avoid confusion, it is important to lay out the areas for which each will be responsible. With respect to roles, there should be a "key person" provision: if certain individuals become unavailable, both parties will be involved with securing a replacement.

Since issues are common within large implementations, a way to raise issues to appropriate personnel within the implementation firm's organization should be agreed upon up front. This escalation policy should be agreed upon with benchmarks of who can be escalated to resolve certain issues within the implementation firm's organization. Contact details like cell phone numbers all the way up to the executive level can be gained through this process. Last, if there is a "system integrator," which can be defined as having ownership of other vendor's deliverables and perhaps even deliverables that are created by the customer, this should be clearly laid out as well.

DELIVERABLES:

Key deliverables should be clearly defined and described in the contract, including who is responsible for the creation of the deliverable and the acceptance criteria. Ideally the parties should agree upon what deliverables look like during the contracting phase. This can be done as an appendix to the contract itself or some other document that is circulated at the time of contract signing.

DATES/TOLLGATES:

While specific hard and fast deadlines sometimes are problematic, having tollgate dates or thresholds is critical. This can be done in two ways: having a tollgate at a set time (e.g., quarterly tollgates to review progress) or when a certain threshold is met (e.g., design is 80 percent complete). It is also a best practice to have a party that is not involved with the implementation perform this review. This reviewer can be vendor management or a committee of individuals who are familiar with implementations but not deployed to the one in scope here.

INCENTIVE CONTRACTS:

As mentioned previously, if this is an incentive/ reward-based contract, one needs to be very explicit as to the terms. These incentives should be tied directly to desired outcomes. They should be measurable, with metrics that are easy to collect. For instance, if one of the incentives were "System test completed by 3/1 with less than 5 percent severity-one issues," one would need to clearly define a severity-one issue in this contract, have adequate input about who classifies issues, and the actual metric (the number of issues found) should be readily collected and communicated.

Post-Contract Monitoring
It is important for someone on the customer side to manage the contractual provisions on an ongoing basis. This is usually done by individuals involved with the implementation but can be done by a vendor management team. This should be done continuously throughout the implementation project, not just at the beginning and the end.

- Dates/Milestones: Any provisions related to dates or milestones should be proactively monitored by a specific individual or a team of individuals for the customer. It should be possible for this monitoring activity to predict ahead of time whether a milestone is going to be missed so plans can be adjusted. If a deadline is missed, it is important to diligently engage at the earliest possible to prevent things from getting worse.

- Status: The status/health of a project should be continuously monitored by the customer's reviewing team. There should be specific criteria that, when met, begin a "rehabilitation" process—for instance, three consecutive statuses in Red, going from Red status to Green back to Red, or three consecutive yellows statuses. The timing and audience for these reviews and the format should be agreed upon during the negotiation phase. It is also important for this reviewing team to critique and review status reports; there are many instances of less-than-accurate status reports being circulated.

- Service Level/Operating Level Agreements: To the extent that they are in the contract, these should be monitored consistently and closely. They should be validated and tracked by the reviewing team for trends. Similar to incentives, these should be readily obtained and drive a desired behavior. There should also be provisions related to SLA review—annually is a common period. Service Level Agreements without "teeth" are those that do not offer any significant penalties to the implementation firm for not meeting the agreed-upon levels. At times, the contract might provide teeth, but are they sharp or dull? Is the penalty to the implementation firm's impact sufficient to drive the desired behavior? The goal is not financial reward but rather guaranteed service levels. Service Level Objectives (SLOs) are advised against. A SLO is ultimately a commitment to do the "best" in case of a failure. There are rarely true commitments with a SLO.

Deliverable Review:

As a part of a tollgate review, or as any other ongoing vendor management, it is important to continue to review deliverables as the project progresses. As timelines compress in an implementation, sometimes sign-off becomes a mere formality. For this reason, it is important to have an objective review team continuously check deliverables for completeness and accuracy.

Staffing:

Turnover on any large scale systems implementation is unavoidable. This will likely occur with both the implementation firm as well as with the customer.

However, when turnover affects key individuals, or the amount of turnover at large gets into the double digits, it would be prudent to consider the root cause of these departures. Many firms, in an effort to reduce third-party risk, investigate firms to determine what might be going on in a implementation firm.

Project Plans and Contracts

This section discusses the intersection between project plans (also known as Work Breakdown Structures [WBS]) and contracting.

DATES:

It is relatively rare to have a complete, detailed, and agreed-upon WBS in the contracting phase, but the parties typically agree upon key dates, like the end date, or implementation date. This date should be shared with both parties as early as possible to reduce confusion or surprise. To the extent that other key dates can be agreed on, such as key milestones, these are helpful as well.

OWNERSHIP:

As it relates to the WBS, it is important to detail who will approve, maintain, provide input to, and be communicated with in the contract. The WBS is a key document, and there is usually a direct correlation with who maintains the document and who is in control of the project.

CHANGES:
It is important for the WBS to be a living document. Updating status and estimates, for example, are a key task of project management. However, after a project has been accepted, the process of making changes to completion dates must be formalized and detailed in writing. This is important to document as it adds a degree of formality and seriousness to date revisions.

Conclusion
While there may be no magic bullet contract, Statement of Work, or Master Services Agreement that guarantees a project's success, there are those documents that start the project out on the right foot by being specific and well thought out, with effective monitoring and communication.

Overview and Next Steps

If you are a customer of an implementer,
the key takeaways from this book are:

1. Have detailed, documented roles between yourself and your implementation partner.

2. Be active in the areas of requirements definition and testing. Deploy the right number of resources with the right skills to these areas.

3. Have a strong, involved change agent.

4. Document, document, document, especially when changes are introduced.

If you are an implementation firm, *the key takeaways from this book are:*

1. Assume everything produced will be discovered in any subsequent litigation.

2. Speak up if you feel the requirements are not concise. If you don't have the right resources from the customer, communicate to them and document the situation.

3. Be particularly careful around change requests. Have a consistent methodology for change governance.

4. Note the importance of active sign-offs from your customer.

If you are an attorney representing either a customer of an implementation firm or the firm itself, *the key takeaways from the book are:*

1. Engage your technology experts sooner than you would normally engage an expert. Given the intricacies and complexities in these cases, you can't engage an expert too soon.

2. Get familiar with the technology terms and phrases presented in Section 3.1, "Technology Primer for Attorneys," page 52.

3. Understand that these cases are usually not black and white. There is usually no single best way to solve a problem, nor are any two solutions exactly the same. There is as much art as there is science in any large systems implementation. In other words, different implementations can take completely different paths and still arrive at the desired destination.

Contact Us

Hopefully by now you have a solid understanding of the complexities of Systems Implementation. Over the past several decades I have spent years studying, implementing, planning, executing, and observing the best practices organizations use.

If you would like an expert team to assist you in long- or short-term consulting, answering questions, or as an expert witness, reach out to our team today.

Cases and Outcomes
We've Participated In

Large Technology Programs:
Advises companies and leads large complex program implementations, including core banking, commercial banking, ERP, and payments technologies. Troubleshoots, corrects, and provides expert witness analysis and testimony.

Target Operating Models:
Performs operational and technology analyses to identify opportunities within organizations to optimize their use of people, business processes, and technology in a consistent manner.

Operational/Risk Effectiveness and Process Re-Engineering:

Advises senior operations and technology executives on transforming organizations to improve performance and reduce expenses, as well as risk, through business process automation. Specializes in assessing operational, compliance, and strategic risks; opines on management responses and corresponding control activities.

Large Technology Programs

Has conducted over a dozen large post-implementation reviews that will culminate in root cause analysis and potential expert witness reports and testimony.

These original engagements accumulated over $4 billion in technology spending.

Led the effort to create a program delivery methodology for a large US card issuer and bank's largest initiative to reduce failure rates and implementation costs.

The resulting methodology and team were put in place to manage the PMO for a large engagement for the client.

Implemented a ticketless transaction system to significantly reduce transaction times and costs in the branch environment of a large US bank.

Once deployed, this system removed 85 percent of paper through the use of point-of-sale devices.

Led several cross-functional and highly integrated ERP-related initiatives around G/L and related accounting systems. One of these initiatives was over $200 million in spending.

Led several core banking and commercial systems implementations for Top 10 global banks. These systems were a combination of commercial off-the-shelf (COTS) and custom implementations. These implementations spanned the full spectrum of banking activities.

Led the creation of completely customized solutions in core banking, commercial banking, payments, mortgage banking, and mortgage servicing.

Target Operating Models:

Led the deployment of multiple enterprise target operating models for several Top 10 global banks. Analyzed the overarching business strategies and aligned these strategies with the future state technology architecture and the application portfolio.

Recommended organizational models, enterprise architecture, and process improvements, which reduced delivery and support costs.

Led several related engagements at two large European banks and two US midsized investment management firms to assess and rationalize their use of various infrastructure technologies to reduce costs and increase system availability.

Employed strategies including virtualization, systems management investments, and process outsourcing.

Operational/Risk Effectiveness and Process Re-engineering

Conducted several IT risk and compliance assessments, which included the technology remediation required to comply with various regulations (GLBA, UDAP, FFIEC, etc.)

Conducted several process re-engineering exercises related to branch processing, payments processing, mortgage processing, credit reporting, risk reporting, and other areas within retail and commercial banking.

Led an effort at a regional bank to retool branch and back-office processes to reduce costs and increase service delivery. Retooled the end-to-end business processes as well as the data center strategy to take a post-disaster scenario into account for ongoing business continuity.

About the Author

Greg Crouse is a global expert in large-scale systems implementations. He has extensive experience remediating systems that get into trouble, as well as being involved with resulting litigation if rescue is impossible.

As the Executive Vice-President of Financial Services and Dispute Services at Mindseeker, Greg has more than twenty-five years of consulting experience in the financial services, manufacturing, and energy industries, with an expertise in payments, technology, business alignment, and operational performance and transformation.

Over the past several decades, Greg has managed key strategic and operational initiatives on several complex integrations for large, multi-national banks, of which many were in excess of $100 million.

His extensive experience integrating business operations with technology are complemented by a deep understanding of core, retail, ERP, financial, and commercial banking systems.

This experience has allowed Greg to troubleshoot and correct some of the largest systems implementations in the world.

Greg has led large, cross-functional, high-performing teams by setting clear strategic vision and solving complex problems in a multitude of delivery models

He advises attorneys in complex commercial litigation that arises out of failed implementation projects.

www.ingramcontent.com/pod-product-compliance
Lightning Source LLC
Chambersburg PA
CBHW032005180326
41458CB00057B/6941